Learning to draw & drawing to learn

DRAWING
The Ancient ROMANS

Author: Max Marlborough works as a freelance author, illustrator and designer of art guides for readers of all ages.

Artist: Mark Bergin was born in Hastings in 1961. He studied at Eastbourne College of Art and has specialised in historical reconstructions as well as aviation and maritime subjects since 1983. He lives in Bexhill-on-Sea with his wife and three children.

Editor: Nick Pierce

Photograph credits:
p14 Marzolino/Shutterstock.com, p36 spatuletail/ Shutterstock.com, p40 Jeff Dalton/Shutterstock.com, p44 Neveshkin Nikolay/Shutterstock.com p45 Constantin SinCo/Shutterstock.com, p48 mountainpix/Shutterstock. com, p48n Mauro Carli/Shutterstock.com, p53 RODKARV/ Shutterstock.com, Philippe PATERNOLLI/Shutterstock.com

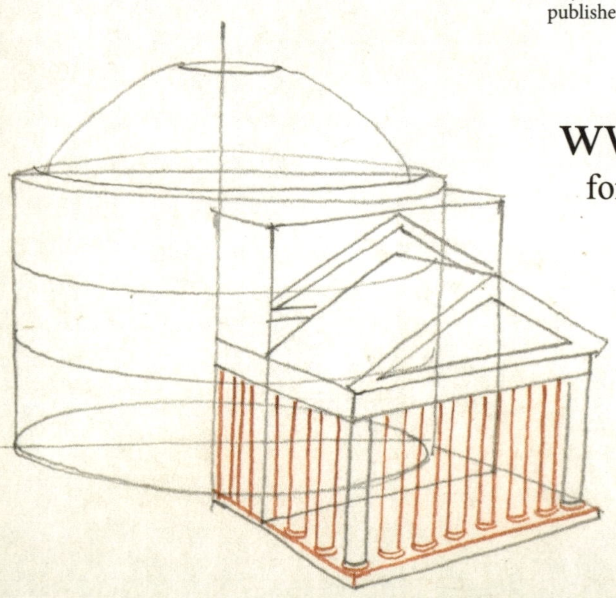

Published in Great Britain in MMXX by
Book House, an imprint of
The Salariya Book Company Ltd
25 Marlborough Place, Brighton BN1 1UB
www.salariya.com

ISBN: 978-1-912904-12-9

SALARIYA
SCRIBO BOOK HOUSE SCRIBBLERS

1 3 5 7 9 8 6 4 2

A CIP catalogue record for this book is available from the British Library.

Printed and bound in China.

Learning to draw & drawing to learn

DRAWING The Ancient ROMANS

Written by

MAX MARLBOROUGH

Illustrated by

MARK BERGIN

BOOK HOUSE

a SALARIYA imprint

CONTENTS

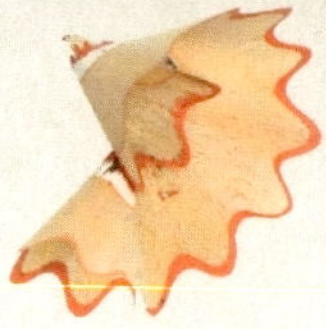

INTRODUCTION

The Ancient Romans ruled over one of the largest and most powerful empires in history. Between the 3rd Century BC and the 5th Century AD, Rome was the centre of the Roman Empire. The lands controlled by the Romans included parts of Europe, including Gaul (France), Greece and Spain, parts of North Africa and parts of the Middle East.

The Ancient Romans are people who originated from different tribes. Over time the largest of the tribes, the 'Latins', became the most dominant. They lived in villages on a group of seven hills overlooking the Tiber River. These villages grew into the city of Rome.

A modern map of the area encompassing the Roman Empire.

MAKING A MAP

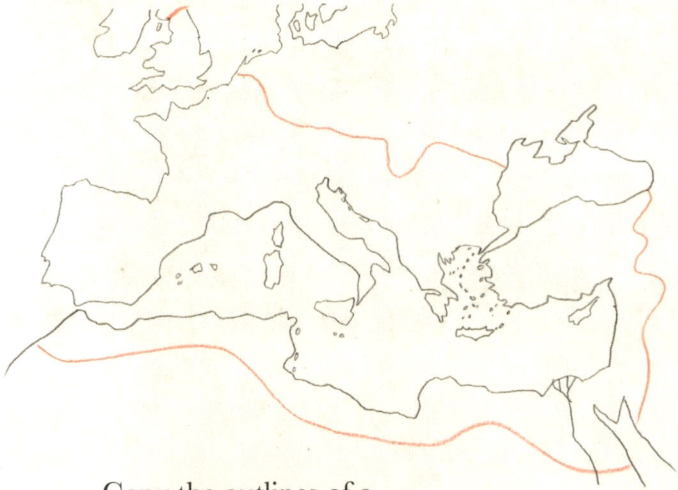

Copy the outlines of a map of the area.

Design small Roman icons to place on your map.

Add details to your map and a border to make it look like it's on parchment.

MATERIALS

PAPER

Bristol paper is good for crayons, pastels and felt-tip pens. Watercolour paper is thicker; it is the best choice for water-based paints or inks.

PENCILS

Try out different grades of pencils. Hard pencils make fine grey lines and soft pencils make softer, darker marks.

PAINTS

Ordinary watercolours are translucent (see-through); gouache is not. Try other kinds of paints, too.

FELT-TIP PENS

Felt-tips usually come in sets of mixed colours. The ones that make very thin lines are called fineliners.

STYLES

Try using different types of drawing paper and materials. Experiment with charcoal, wax crayons and pastels. All pens, from felt-tips to ballpoints, will make interesting marks – you could also try drawing with pen and ink on wet paper.

Cameo

Ink pen

Gladiator helmet

It can be tricky adding light and shade with an **ink** pen. Analyse your drawing. The lightest areas should be left untouched. Then apply solid areas of ink to the darkest parts. The midtones are achieved by hatching (single parallel lines) or cross-hatching (criss-crossed lines).

Lines drawn in **ink** cannot be erased, so keep your ink drawings sketchy and less rigid. Don't worry about mistakes as these lines can be lost in the drawing as it develops.

Silhouette of Roman soldier carrying a standard

Ancient Roman triumphal arch

Pencil

Hard pencils are greyer and soft pencils are blacker. Hard pencils are usually graded from 6H (the hardest) through 5H, 4H, 3H and 2H to H.

Soft pencils are graded from B, 2B, 3B, 4B and 5B up to 6B (the softest).

Silhouette

Silhouette is a style of drawing that uses only a solid black shape.

Roman mosaic of a dragon

PERSPECTIVE

If you look at any object from different viewpoints, you will see that the part that is closest to you looks larger, and the part furthest away from you looks smaller. Drawing in perspective is a way of creating a feeling of depth – of showing three dimensions on a flat surface.

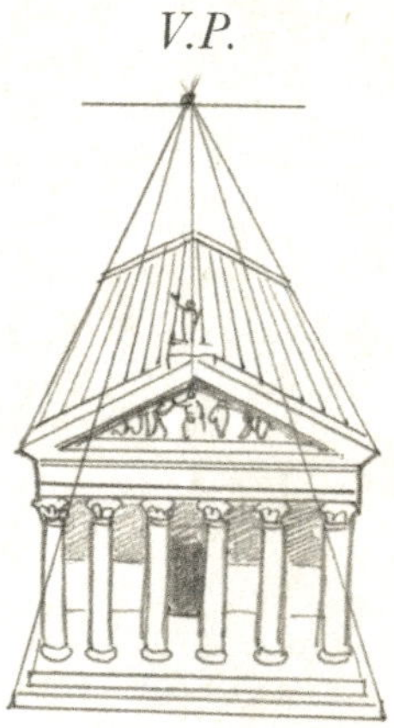

The vanishing point (V.P.) is the place in a perspective drawing where parallel lines appear to meet. The position of the vanishing point depends on the viewer's eye level. Sometimes an unusually high or low viewpoint can give your drawing added drama.

Single-point perspective uses one V.P. – a single reference point where lines converge to create a sense of background and foreground.

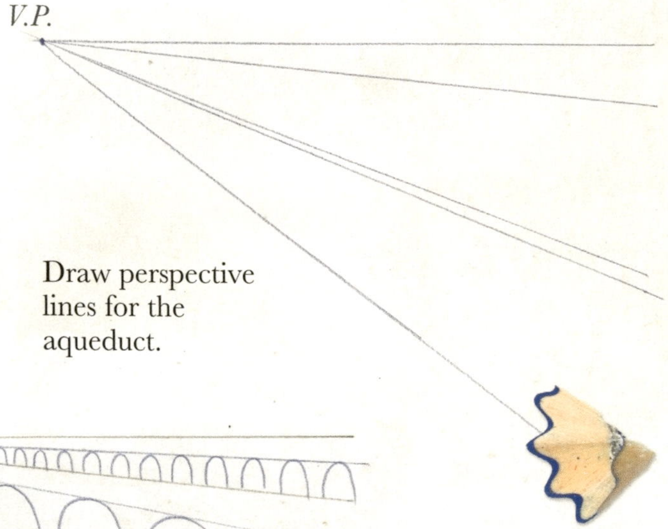

Draw perspective lines for the aqueduct.

Draw in the arches of the aqueduct, making them incrementally larger as they get closer.

Draw the inside edge of each arch.

Draw in some surrounding countryside.

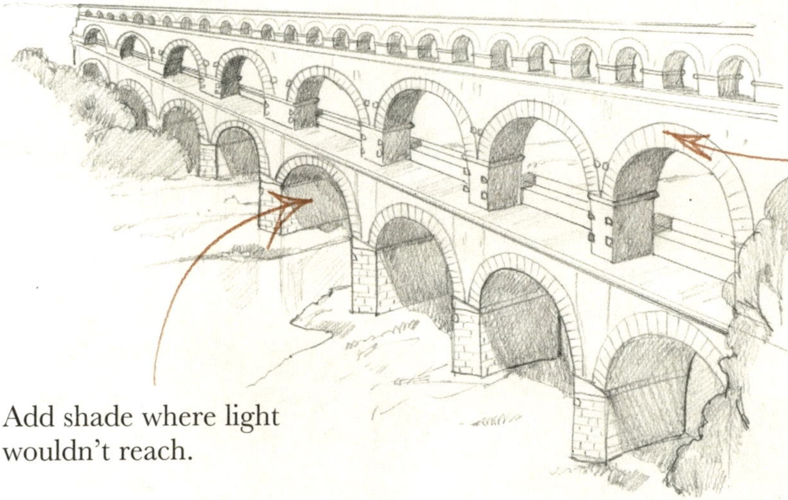

Complete any remaining detail.

Erase any unwanted construction lines.

Add shade where light wouldn't reach.

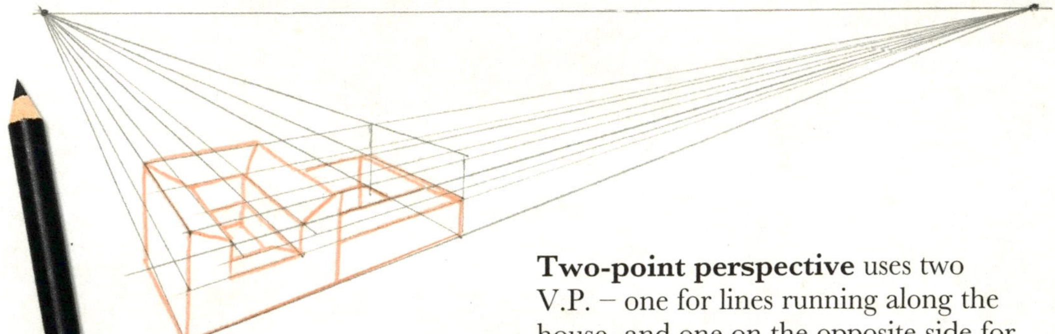

Two-point perspective uses two V.P. – one for lines running along the house, and one on the opposite side for lines running across the house. (Use this technique to draw the house on p.56.)

ROMAN TEMPLES

The Pantheon was completed in the reign of the Emperor Hadrian around 125 AD. It is one of the best known and best preserved ancient Roman buildings in Rome today.

Postage stamp showing the Pantheon.

When buildings and monuments had been rebuilt, Emperor Hadrian made a practice of dedicating them in honour of the original builder. The Pantheon was dedicated to Marcus Agrippa. The prominent inscription on the façade of the porch reads: M. AGRIPPA L.F. COS TERTIUM FECIT (Marcus Agrippa, son of Lucius, three-time consul, made this.)

The Pantheon's dome is still the world's largest unreinforced concrete dome. The oculus, which is the opening at the top of the dome, is 8.2 m (27 feet) in diameter. Striking patterns of sunlight illuminate the walls and floors of porphyry, granite and yellow marbles.

View of the ancient Roman temple Maison Carrée during a sunny morning in Nîmes in the Occitanie region of southern France.

Facade of the Library of Celsus, an ancient Roman building in Ephesus, Anatolia. It is a popular tourist attraction.

HOW TO DRAW THE PANTHEON

The name Pantheon means 'of, relating to, or common to all the gods' in ancient Greek. It is thought that the name comes from the statues of many gods placed around this building or the dome opening onto the heavens.

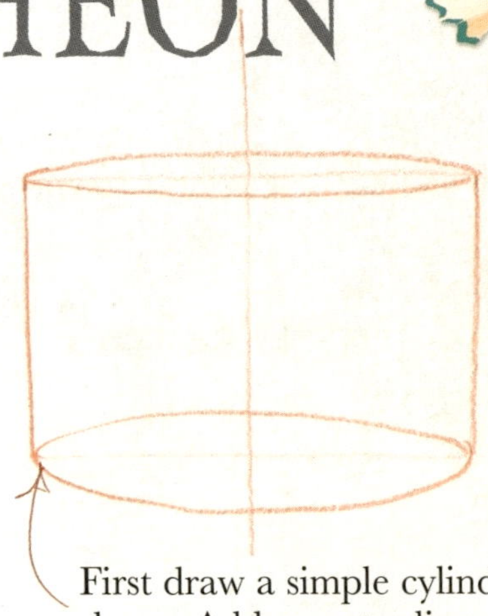

First draw a simple cylinder shape. Add a centre line.

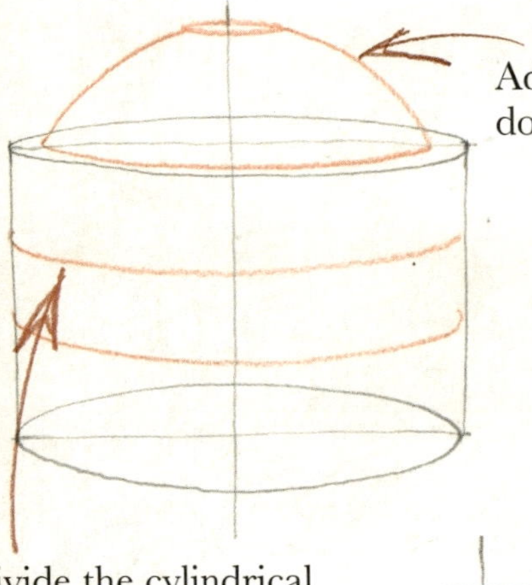

Add a domed roof.

Divide the cylindrical building into sections.

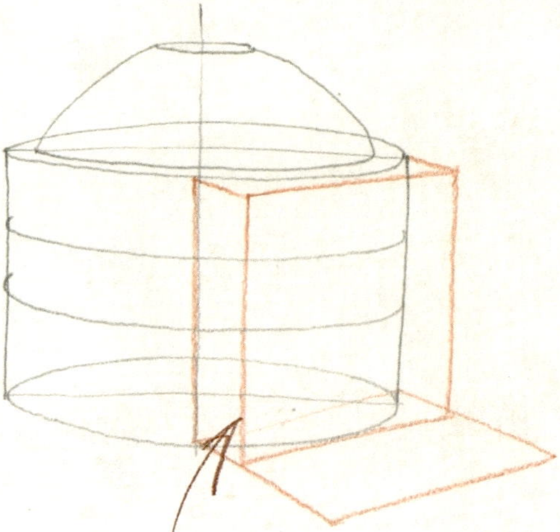

Draw a box shape for the facade of the building.

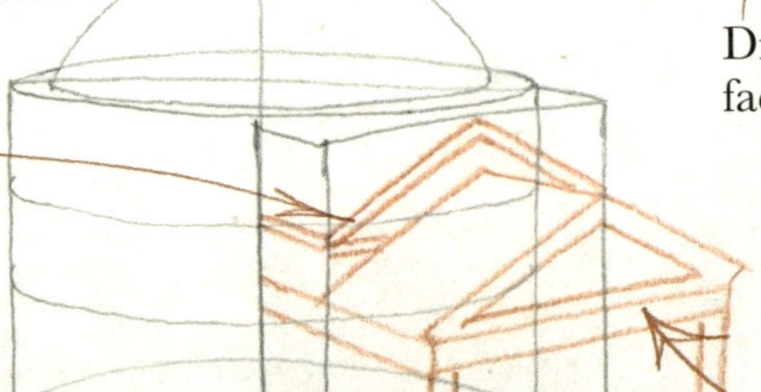

Add a triangle shape to the facade.

Draw in the front roofed section of the building.

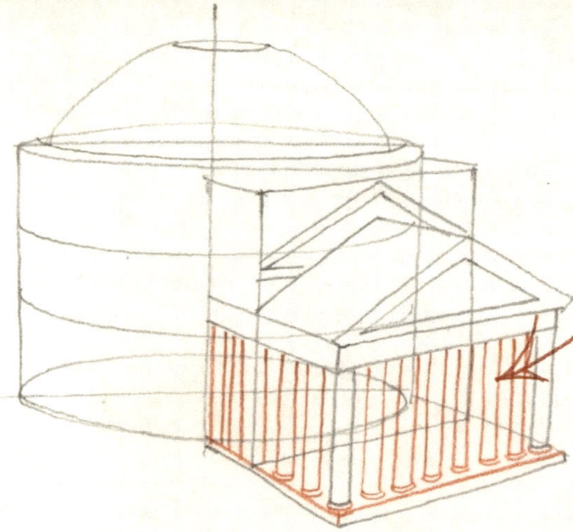

Draw columns lining the front section of the building.

Add sections to the roof.

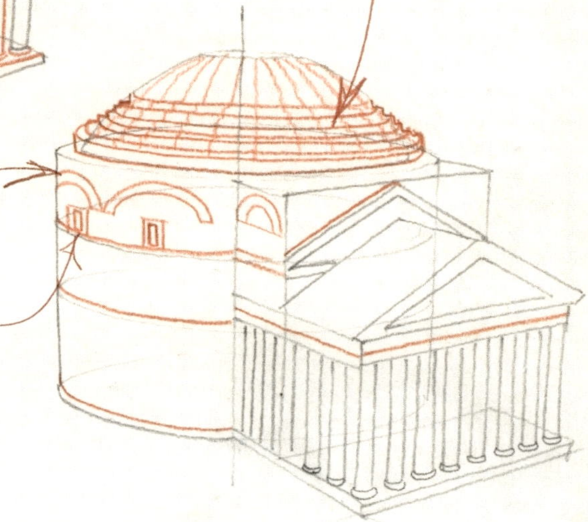

Add the arch designs.

Add windows.

Complete all remaining details.

Decide on your light source before you start adding any shading.

Draw in roof tiles.

Add an inscription to the front of the building.

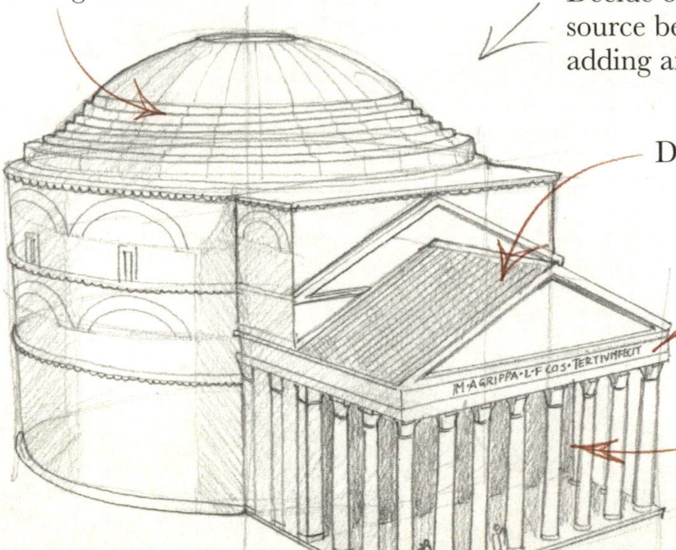

Add shading to areas light wouldn't reach.

Erase any unwanted construction lines.

PHOTOGRAPHS

Drawing from photographs can help you identify shape and form and will help you to draw more accurately. Be careful to choose photographs which haven't been distorted by camera angles or lenses.

Statue of Caesar at the Forum of Augustus, Italy.

Choose a good photograph and trace it.

Mark out a squared grid over your traced drawing to divide your drawing into small sections.

Lightly draw a squared grid of the same proportions on your drawing paper. You can now transfer the shapes from each square of the tracing paper to your drawing paper.

To make your drawing look three-dimensional, decide which side the light source is coming from, and add areas of shadow where the light doesn't reach.

Sketch in an overall tone and add surrounding textures to create interest and a sense of movement. Think about how you position your drawing on the paper; this is called composition.

WORSHIP

The people of the Roman Empire recognised and worshipped multiple gods and goddesses. Romans worshipped in public and at home. Roman homes were protected by household gods – the lares, who were the family's ancestral spirits, and the penates, who looked after the larder. They were worshipped every day at the household shrine, the lararium. The public gods were those of the official state religion. Many of these were based on Greek gods which the Romans had adopted.

Some gods, such as Mithras – a god popular with soldiers – originally came from regions that had been conquered by the Romans. The secretive cult of Mithras began in Persia. Some gods were only worshipped locally.

HOW TO DRAW THE GODS

People in the provinces were allowed to carry on worshipping their own local gods as long as they also worshipped the Roman state gods. Some Romans found the state religion too impersonal and turned to cults from the east which seemed more positive.

THE ROMAN GODS

The Roman gods included:

- **Jupiter,** king of the gods and god of the sky, thunder and lightning. His special symbols were an eagle or a thunderbolt.
- **Juno,** sister and wife of Jupiter. She was the goddess of women and of childbirth. Her special symbol was a peacock.
- **Mars,** god of war. He wore the armour and weapons of a soldier. The month of March is named after him.
- **Bacchus,** god of wine. He was one of the most popular gods. His symbol was a bunch of grapes.
- **Pan,** god of the mountains. He was one of the Greek gods that the Romans adopted. Half man, half goat, he always appeared with his pipes.
- **Minerva,** goddess of wisdom, war and crafts. She was shown with a helmet and spear.
- **Neptune,** god of the sea and freshwater. He was often depicted carrying a trident.
- **Isis,** the goddess of motherhood, nature and magic. She was originally an Egyptian goddess.
- **Mithras** was the god at the centre of a secretive cult which had started in Persia.
- **Venus,** the goddess of love and beauty.
- **Diana,** goddess of the Moon and hunting.
- **Pluto,** god of the Underworld. His counterpart in Greek mythology was Hades.

THE ROMAN GODS

ROMAN MYTHS AND LEGENDS

The ancient Romans believed that the gods helped with the founding of the city of Rome. Mars and a Vestal Virgin named Rhea Silvia were the parents of twin boys: Romulus and Remus. Vestal Virgins were not allowed to marry or have children but had to devote their lives to serving Vesta, the goddess of the fire and hearth.

It is said that King Amulius ordered that the twins be thrown into the Tiber River as a punishment to Rhea Silvia for betraying her vows. Fortunately, the boys were rescued from the river Tiber by a female wolf who helped to raise the boys until a local couple found and adopted them. As the boys grew up, they overthrew King Amulius and together they established a new city. Later, Romulus killed his brother Remus and went on to name the city after himself, calling it Rome (or Roma).

Zeus, the supreme god of the ancient Greeks, was known to the Romans as Jupiter. In this Roman wall painting, Victory crowns him with bay leaves. The eagle and globe at his feet are symbols of his greatness.

HOW TO DRAW MYTHS AND LEGENDS

The image of the she-wolf suckling Romulus and Remus has been a symbol of Rome since ancient times and is one of the most recognisable icons of ancient mythology.

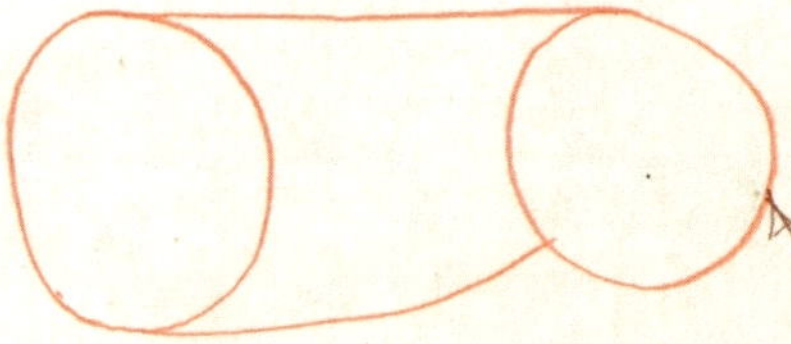

First draw two ovals joined together for the main body (as shown).

Draw in the wolf's head shape and add facial features.

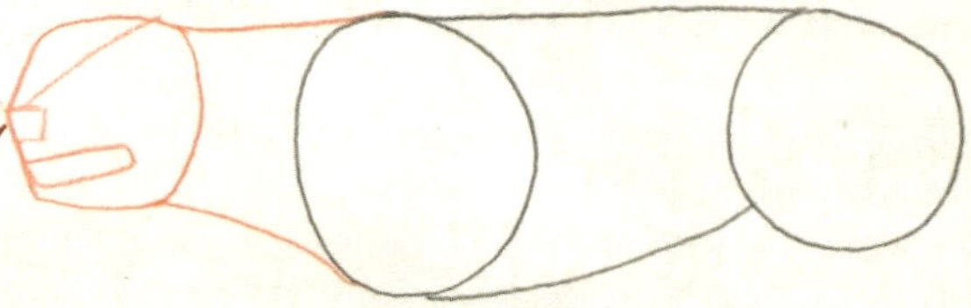

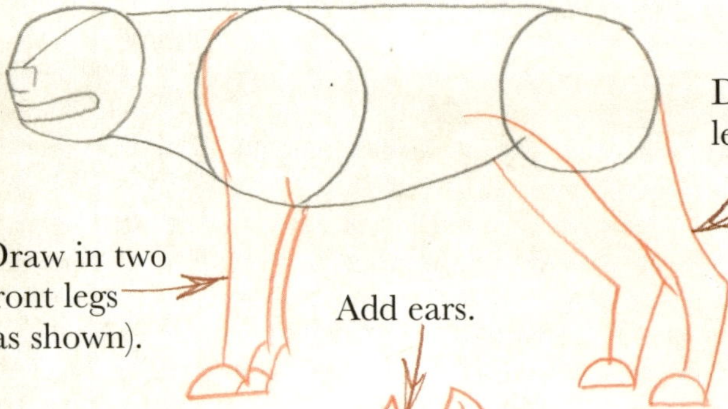

Draw in two hind legs (as shown).

Draw in two front legs (as shown).

Add ears.

Add lines to indicate the wolf's ribs.

Add the tail.

Add the nose.

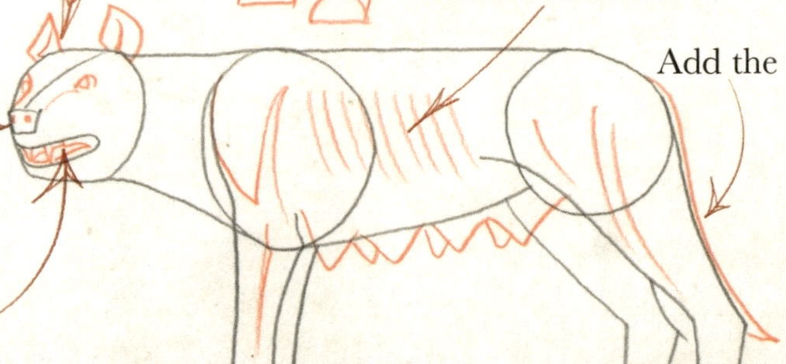

Draw in the mouth and add sharp teeth.

Draw in basic shapes for the bodies and the heads of Romulus and Remus.

Add arms and legs to the two infants.

The infants' heads should be drawn at an angle (as shown).

Complete all remaining details.

Add muscles to the body.

Use tone to give the head shape.

Add shade to areas light wouldn't reach.

Erase any unwanted construction lines.

HOW TO DRAW ROMAN POTTERY

Pottery was produced in vast quantities in ancient Rome, mostly for everyday use. It was used all over the Roman Empire. Pottery is a key material in the dating and interpretation of archaeological sites.

Draw the general shape of each pot. It can be helpful to draw a centre line to work from.

Add bases to the pots.

Add a handle on each side of the pot.

Draw in a high curved handle.

Add lines to indicate the decorative areas of each pot.

Add a line around the lip.

Draw in patterned borders.

Draw in figurative decorations.

Draw animal decorations.

Complete all the remaining details.

Leave areas of white for highlights.

Add dark tone to areas light wouldn't reach.

Add shadows beneath the vases.

Add a handle.

Add a ship design.

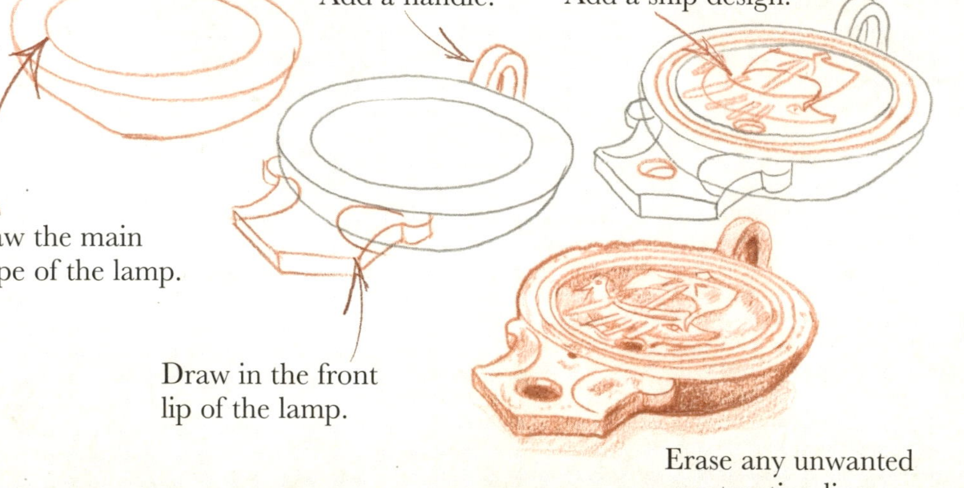

Draw the main shape of the lamp.

Draw in the front lip of the lamp.

Erase any unwanted construction lines.

ROMAN BOWL

Most busy streets in Rome were lined with shops and workshops. The shops opened out on to the street, while the craftsmen worked in the area at the back. A great variety of craftsmen were needed to keep the city supplied with goods. There were smiths, potters, sculptors, glass blowers, carpenters, masons, bone carvers and many more.

Start by drawing a large rectangle.

Draw a second horizontal line at the top. Add vertical lines.

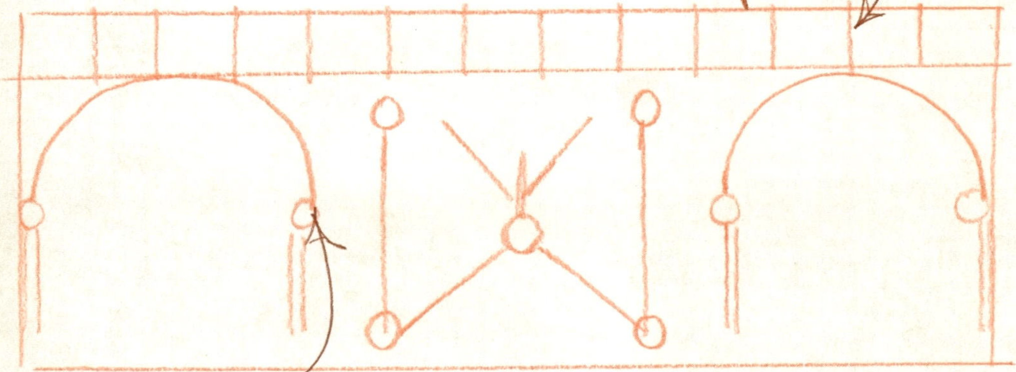

Draw in two arches.

Mark in the structure for the floral design.

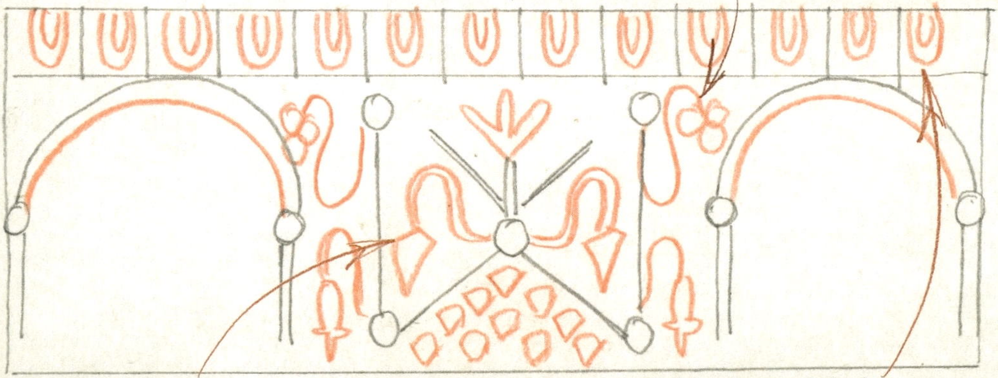

Now add shapes to the floral design.

Add a looped design to each box section.

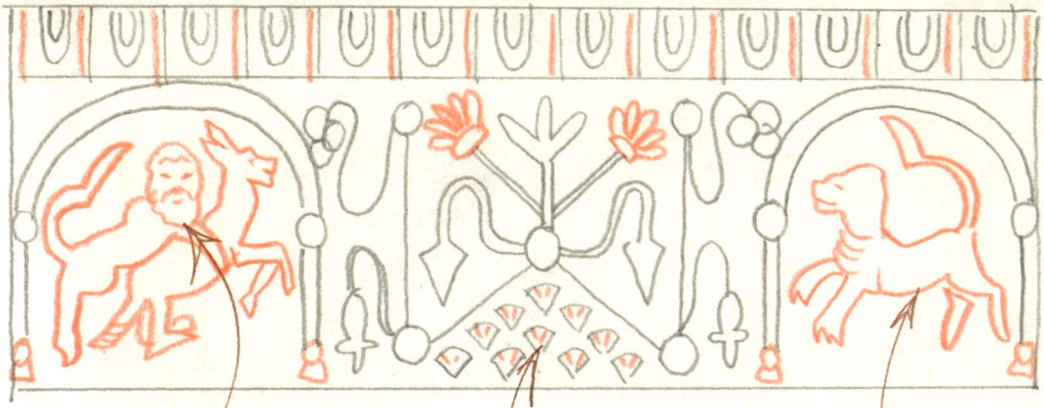

Draw a lion attacking its prey.

Complete the floral design.

Draw another lion.

Draw in the top and base of the bowl (as shown). Using the side of your pencil, add a textured surface to the bowl.

Complete all remaining details.

Add dark tone to areas light wouldn't reach.

Erase any unwanted construction lines.

ROMAN FOOD

Rich ancient Romans liked to invite their friends to banquets. Serving exotic food, they often hired a master-chef to cook these special meals. Guests arrived in the late afternoon and spent all evening reclining on couches in the 'triclinium' (dining room). Romans considered nine to be the ideal number of guests. There were always three couches: one for family members and two for the guests. Ordinary people ate cheaper food: bread porridge, olives, onions, garlic, cheese, salt fish and fruit. This was a much healthier diet than that eaten by the wealthy.

The main industry of the Roman Empire was farming. As the empire grew and its population increased, a regular food supply was essential. Huge numbers of people, mainly slaves, worked on the land. The Romans grew olives, beans, peas, onions and cabbage. Cabbage was thought to be good for digestion. A staple of poorer Romans' diet was dried peas. As the empire expanded, new vegetables and fruits were imported.

Much of the food eaten by ancient Romans is similar to the food we eat today. They ate meat, fish, vegetables, eggs, cheese, grains and different kinds of beans. Meat included animals like dormice (an expensive delicacy), hare, snails and boar. Smaller birds like thrushes were eaten, as well as chickens and pheasants. Beef was not popular with the Romans and any farmed meat was a luxury. Game was much more common. Meat was usually boiled or fried – ovens were rare.

For the ordinary Roman, lentaculum was breakfast, served at daybreak. A small lunch, prandium, was eaten at around 11am. Cena was the main meal of the day. They may have eaten a late supper called vesperna.

HOW TO DRAW ANCIENT MOSAICS

Ancient Roman mosaics are small square-shaped blocks, usually made from stone or, occasionally, small pebbles, glass or marble called tesserae. Using many different colours, craftsmen created images on floors, walls and roofs.

Draw a square frame. Add the basic shapes of food inside it.

Add herbs and a plucked bird.

Draw in the fish heads.

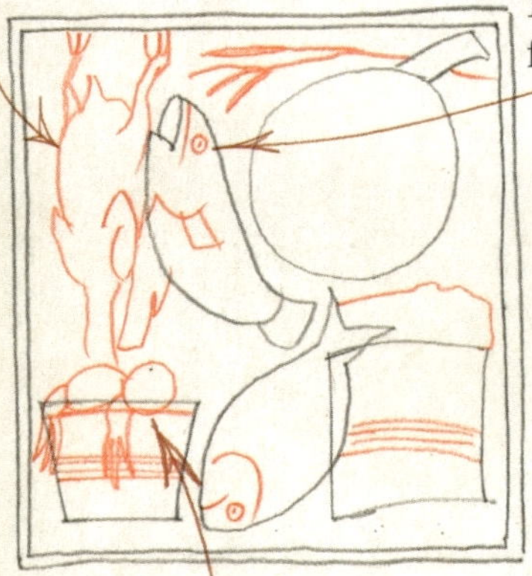

Draw in seafood.

Draw in the figs.

Add detail to the baskets.

Add tone and complete all remaining details.

Erase any unwanted construction lines.

Examples of ancient Roman clothes:

Draw a rectangle with basic shapes for the three figures.

Draw in a ball.

Add facial features and hair.

Add bikini-like costumes.

Draw in two lines behind.

Complete all remaining details.

Add tone to the drawing.

Erase any unwanted construction lines.

GLADIATORS

Some gladiators were trained fighters, and some may have been prisoners of war, or aristocrats forced to earn a living in a 'kill or be killed' contest. Most gladiators, however, were slaves, former slaves or condemned prisoners. Gladiator contests were gory, yet hugely popular spectacles. They were organised so that the emperors and aristocrats could show off their wealth.

Stamp showing the Colosseum, founded in 70 AD, also known as the Flavian Amphitheatre, in the centre of the city of Rome, Italy. It was the largest amphitheatre at the time and held 50,000 spectators.

These bloody entertainments also took place in honour of victories in battle, or to entertain important visitors, celebrate birthdays or simply to distract the ordinary people from everyday political problems.

A stone relief depicting the gladiators.

The Colosseum

The games were held in massive purpose-built arenas throughout the empire from 105 BC to 404 AD. The arenas held thirty, forty or even fifty thousand spectators eagerly watching exotic animals being hunted, prisoners being executed and religious martyrs being thrown to the lions.

Retiarius and secutor gladiators engage in combat.

The most famous gladiator of all was Spartacus, who led an uprising of gladiators and slaves in 73 BC.

The gladiatorial games came to an end in 404 AD as the Christian religion spread throughout the Roman empire. However, criminals and animals continued to be killed for another century.

HOW TO DRAW GLADIATORS

The name 'gladiator' comes from the Latin *gladiatores*. It is the name of their main weapon, the gladius, or short sword. A wide range of weapons, armour and styles of fighting were used by different types of gladiators. A gladiator's weapons and armour dictated his method of fighting.

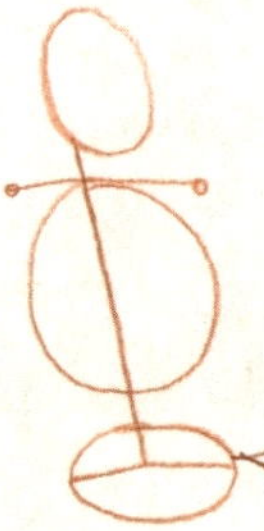

Draw ovals for the head, body and hips. Draw a centre line. Add hip and shoulder lines.

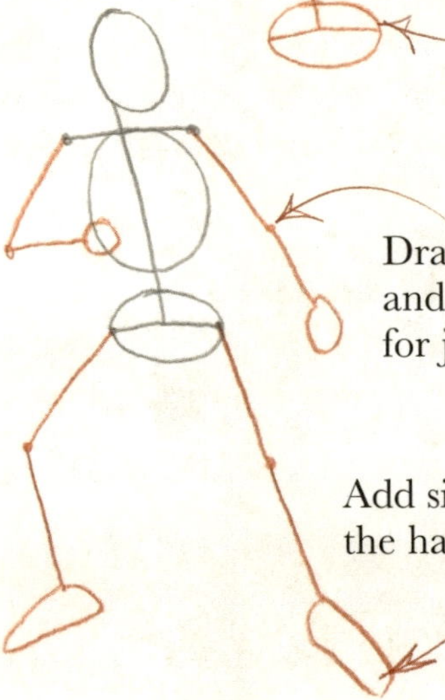

Draw in the arms and legs using dots for joints.

Add simple shapes of the hands and feet.

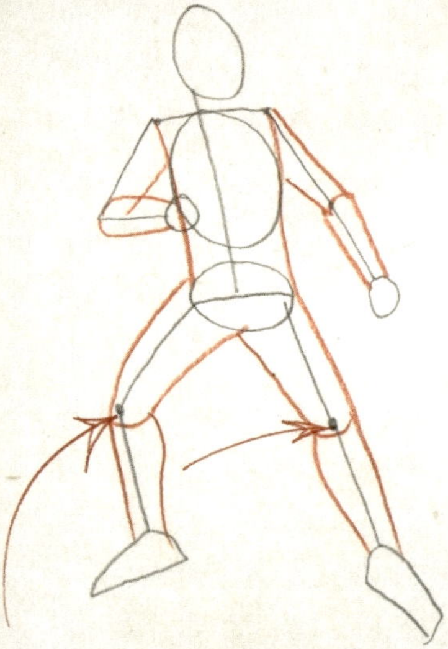

Draw in the shape of the body, legs and arms.

Draw in the helmet.

Add the shield.

Draw in the sword (bent).

Add a loincloth.

Draw in shin guards.

Add a plume and feathers.
Add dots to the face mask.
Draw in the shoulder and arm guard.
Draw in straps and add detail to the loincloth.
Add detail to the shin guard.

Draw in the musculature of the torso.
Add tone to the straps.
Complete all remaining details.
Add shade where light wouldn't reach.

Retiarius
Secutor
Thraex

ROMAN SOLDIERS

The armies of the Roman Empire were well-disciplined and organised. Recruits were taught to march and to think as a single unit, obeying all rules and orders. Ordinary foot soldiers, called legionaries, were all equipped with the same uniform, armour and weapons. Each legionary could carry 40kg (90 lb) for up to 30 km (20 miles) a day. Their training was harsh and punishments for disobedience were severe.

A Roman legionary signed up with the army for 16 years service.

Reconstruction of a legionary helmet. The design was based on a Celtic helmet but had extra features: the sloped neck guard and ear guards, trimmed with brass.

Scene from Trajan's column (above), Rome. Trajan's column was erected to commemorate the successful campaigns of the Emperor Trajan against the Dacian tribes of the Danube frontier in AD 101–102 and 105–106. It stood at the centre of the Emperor's Forum in Rome.

The Roman army was the best trained, best equipped and best organised army in the Roman world. It was divided into legions, each with about 5,500 soldiers. The legion's commander was called a legate. He was assisted by six officers, called tribunes. As the Roman Empire expanded, local tribesmen were recruited to form cohorts. These auxiliary troops backed up the main army.

Gladius (a Roman sword)

HOW TO DRAW ROMAN SOLDIERS

The ancient Roman army consisted of recruits from many different lands. They spoke their own languages, and fought with local weapons, such as bows and arrows and sling-shots.

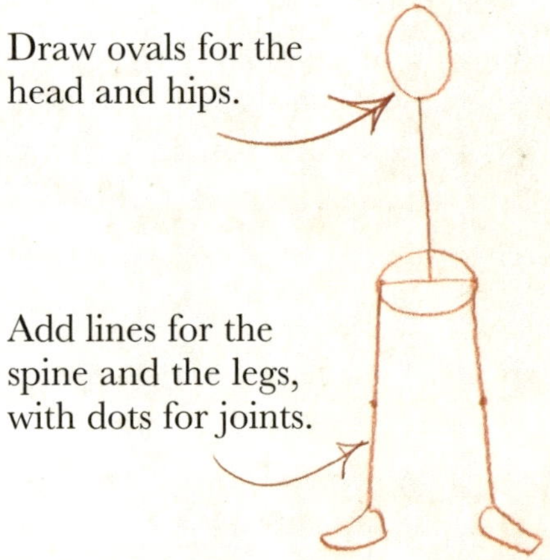

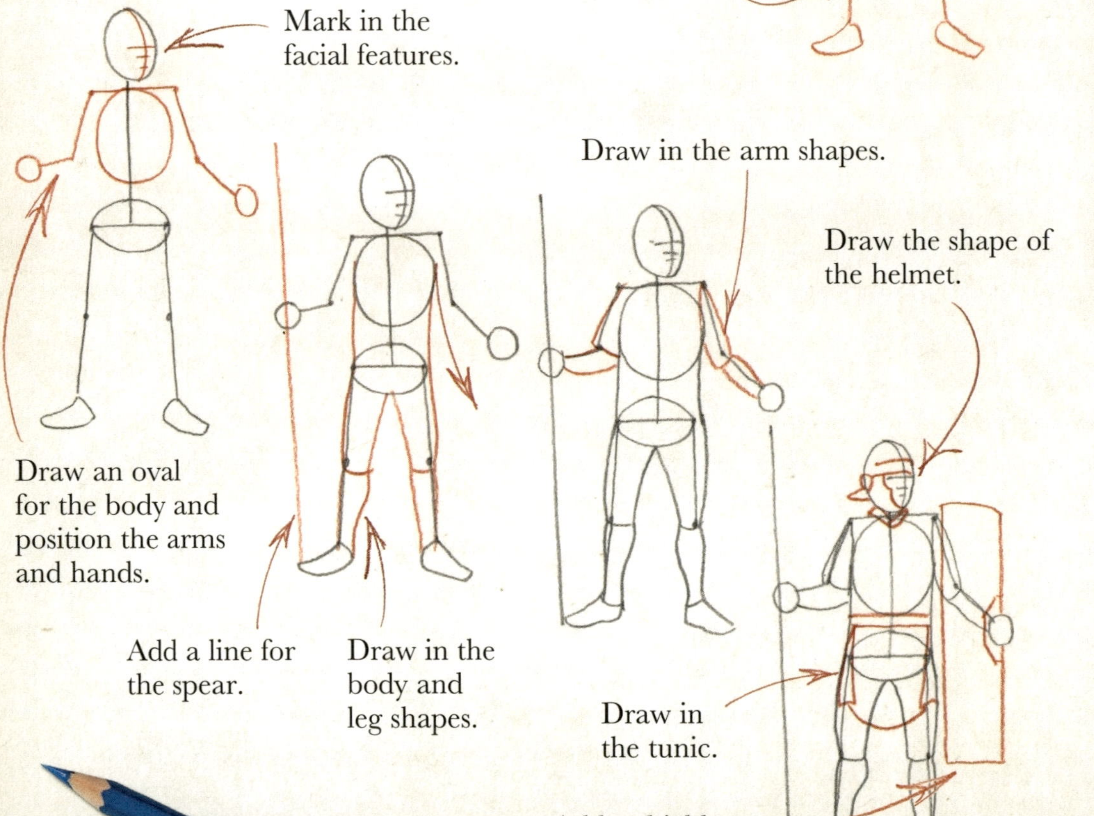

Add a tip to the spear.

Add shoulder armour sections.

Draw in the sword.

Add sandals.

Add detail to the helmet.

Add body armour.

Add detail to the sandals.

Finish the facial details.

Leave areas light for metal highlights.

Complete all remaining details.

Add dark shade to areas light wouldn't reach.

Legate

Erase any unwanted construction lines.

ROMAN SHIPS

Although the Roman navy was instrumental in building the Roman Empire – with the conquest of Britain and the countries surrounding the Mediterranean – its Navy never enjoyed the prestige of the Roman legions. The Romans remained, throughout their history, a land-based people. The Greeks and the Egyptians built ships for the Romans. The Roman Empire grew rich from taxes collected from its many conquered peoples and also through trade.

Merchant ship

Essential foods, especially corn, and many valuable luxury goods were shipped to Rome from distant lands and sold to rich citizens.

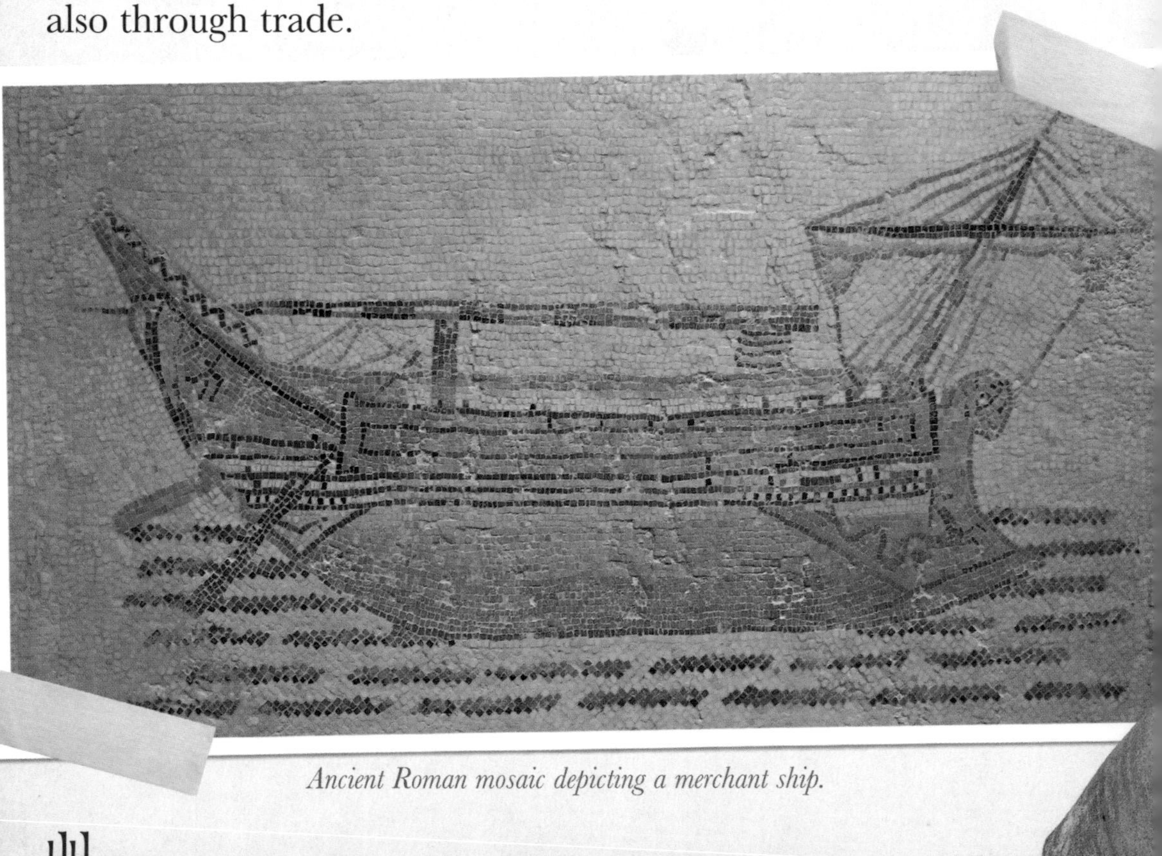

Ancient Roman mosaic depicting a merchant ship.

Ships brought a great variety of goods to Ostia, the harbour for Rome. Huge specially-designed ships brought grain to Rome from Egypt. Most ships were small merchant sailing vessels.

Roman ships' capacity was measured in 'amphorae'. ('amphorae' – a tall ancient Greek or Roman jar or jug with two handles and a narrow neck).

Amphorae

Old Roman boat

HOW TO DRAW A ROMAN SHIP

The merchant ship's main function was to transport cargo. They were built with double planking, which strengthened their hull, allowing them to transport heavy cargo.

Merchant ships anchored at ports, so they did not need a flat hull like warships. Instead, they had a V-shaped hull with ballast, which made them more stable.

Carefully draw the hull of the boat (as shown).

Add the castle.

Draw in the mast.

Draw the swan head.

Add the foremast.

Add the latticed fence.

Add the steering oar.

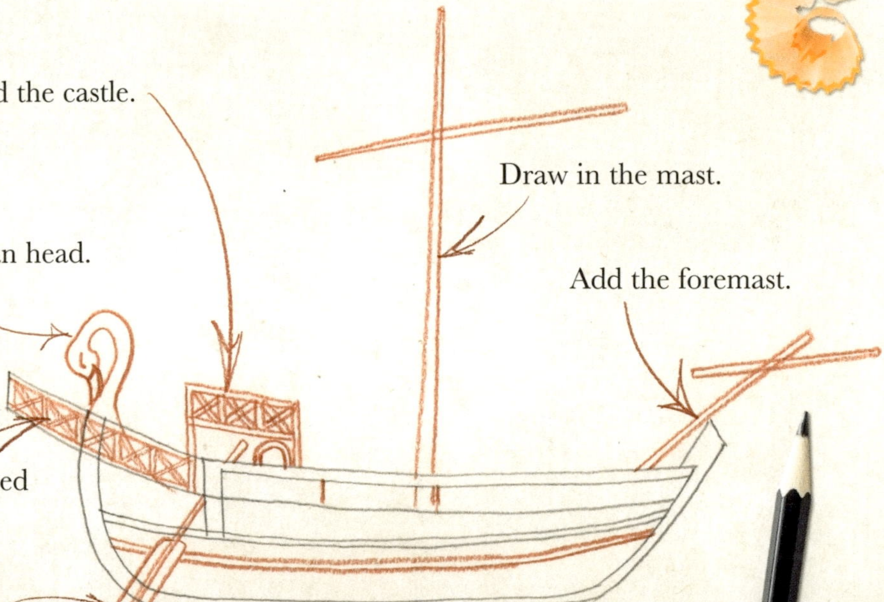

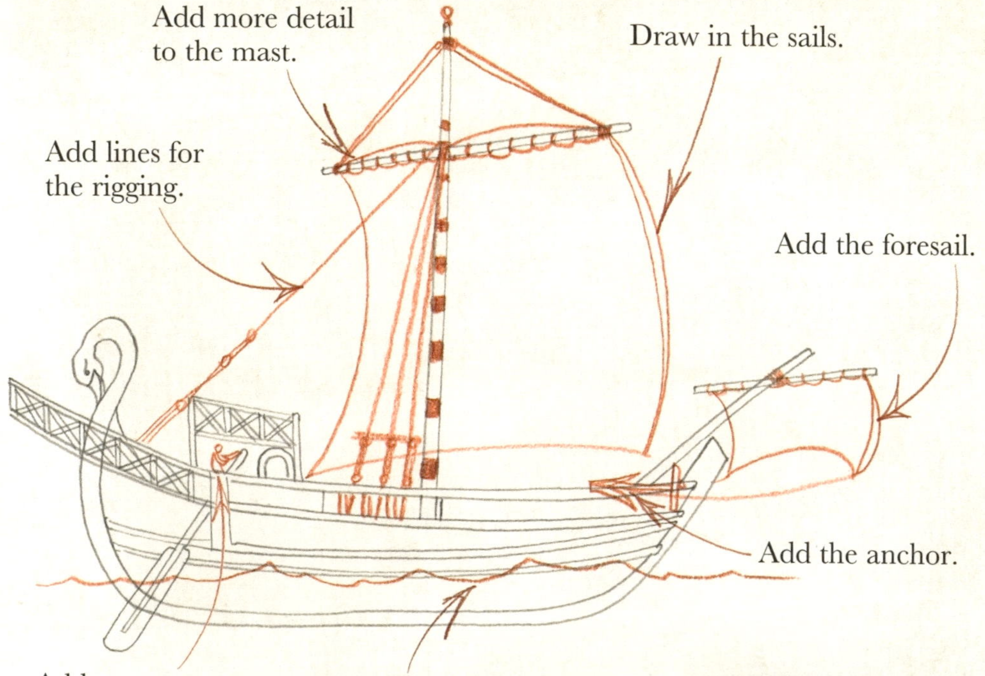
Add more detail to the mast.
Draw in the sails.
Add lines for the rigging.
Add the foresail.
Add the anchor.
Add a person to steer the boat.
Draw in the waves.

Add detail to the sails.
Add more figures.
Draw in lines to indicate wooden structure.
Add shading to the areas light wouldn't reach.
Complete all remaining detail.
Erase any unwanted construction lines.

ROMAN PEOPLE

More than a million people lived in Rome in 100 AD. But they were not all 'freeborn' citizens. Some were foreign merchants, some were people from the empire and very, very many were slaves. Roman law allowed anyone to come and live in the city so long as they could support themselves. But they did not have full citizens' rights. 'Proper' Roman citizens belonged to one of three classes: patricians (nobles), equites (middle rank) or 'plebs', short for ordinary plebeians (ordinary people). Slaves might be prisoners, captured in war or purchased from slave-dealers in nearby lands. Others, the children of slaves, were born unfree.

Many slaves worked as cooks, teachers, doctors and scribes. Some freed by their owners became rich. Most slaves did all the hard or dirty work that their owners would not dream of doing.

Ancient Roman people reenactment

HOW TO DRAW ROMAN FIGURES

There were over 150 different trades in Rome, from wine merchants and goldsmiths to wagon-drivers and bankers. There were also many family-run shops and inns.

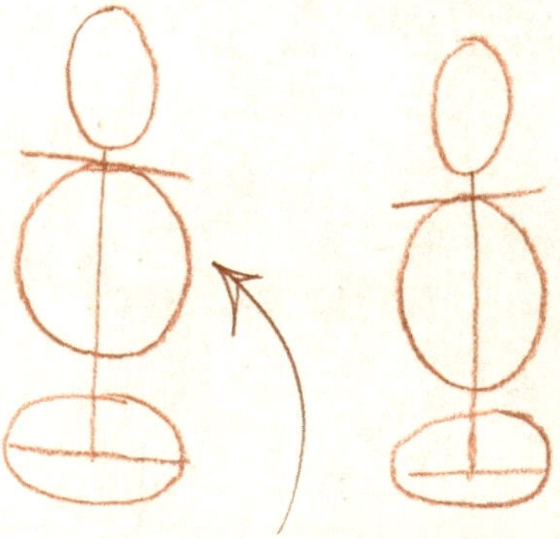

Draw ovals for the heads, bodies and hips. Add a centre line.

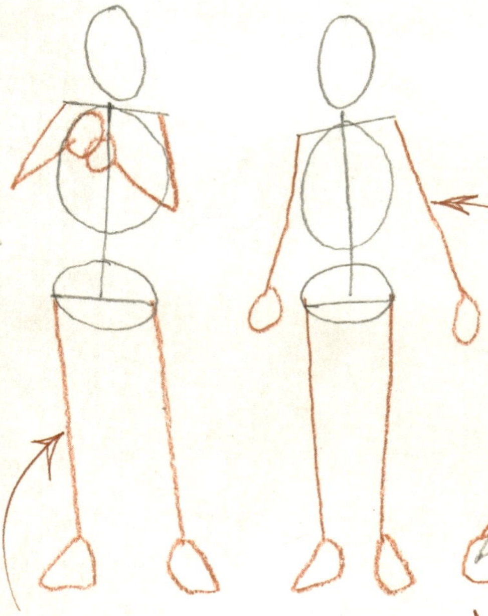

Draw lines for the arms, with dots for joints. Add basic shapes for the hands.

Use lines for the legs and mark in the feet.

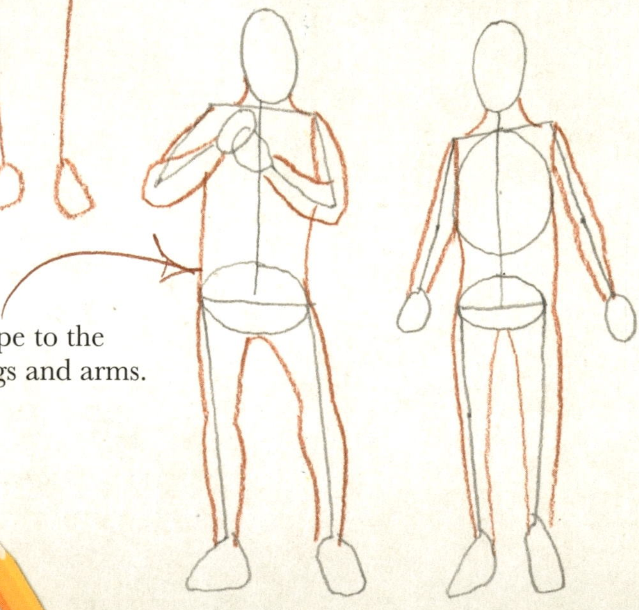

Add shape to the body, legs and arms.

Indicate the facial features.

Draw in the tunic, gathered at the waist.

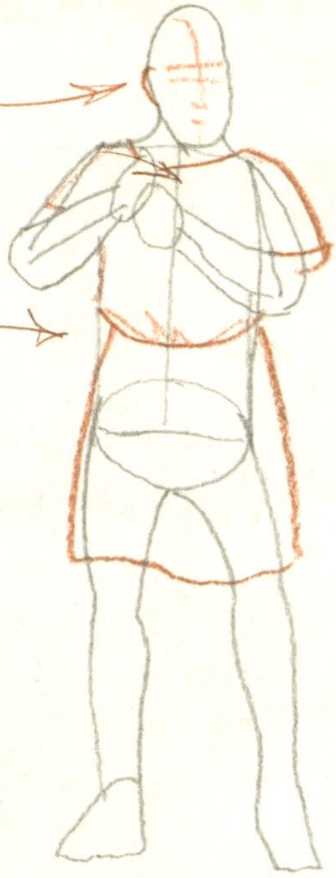

Draw in the dress, gathered at the waist.

Add the long section of dress.

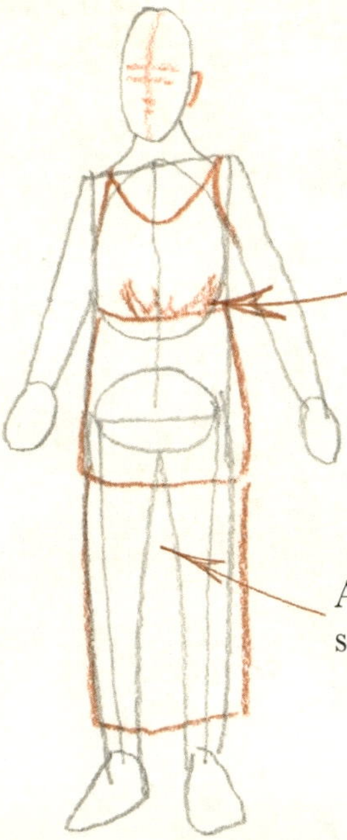

Draw in the facial features and hair.

Add a sack over the man's shoulder.

Add shade to areas light wouldn't reach.

Draw in sandals.

Add folds to the clothing.

Add two buckets.

Erase any unwanted construction lines.

EVERYDAY LIFE

The poet Juvenal said that the Roman people were only interested in 'bread and circuses'. The emperor provided them with 'bread' in the form of free grain and brutal gladiatorial contests were the 'circuses'. The gladiatorial arena takes its name from the sand that was put down to soak up the blood of the men, women and condemned criminals who were forced to fight to entertain the crowds. Gladiator fights, however gory, were hugely popular. They were fights to the death.

Colosseum and Arch of Constantine, Rome, Italy.

The Romans indulged in less brutal relaxations too. The baths were a place to meet friends and relax as well as getting clean.

Ruins of the Baths of Caracalla (Terme di Caracalla), Rome.

HOW TO DRAW ROMAN FURNITURE

Roman furniture varied from the simple and functional to the highly ornate. Chairs and beds were usually made of wood, although some made of metal have survived.

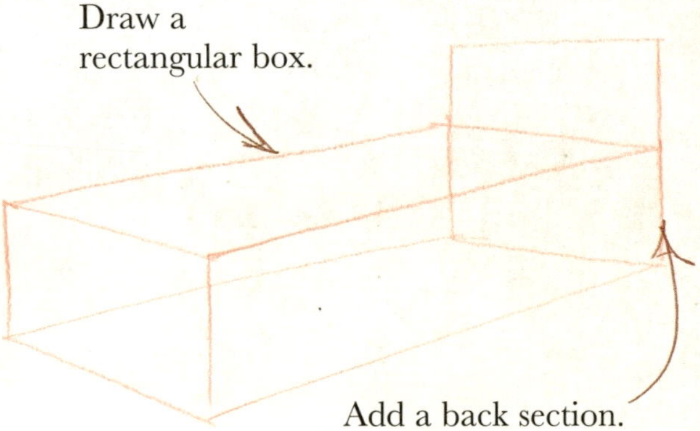

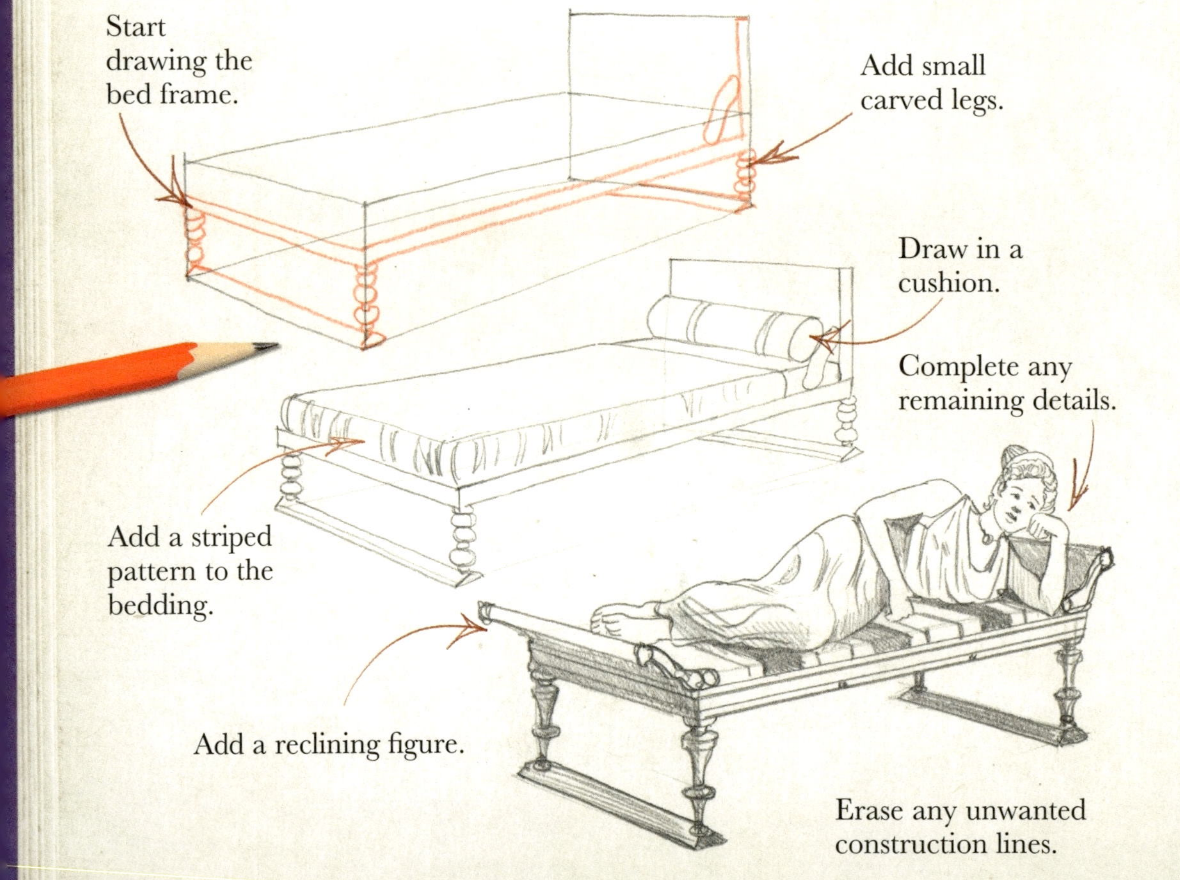

Draw construction lines (as shown) to make an x-shaped folding chair.

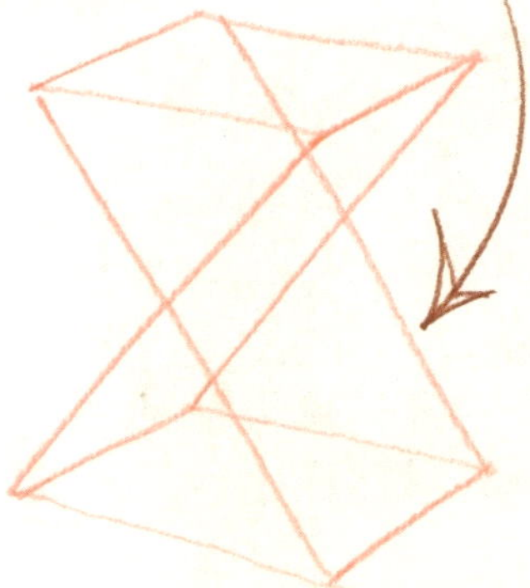

Draw in the chair legs, jointed at the centre.

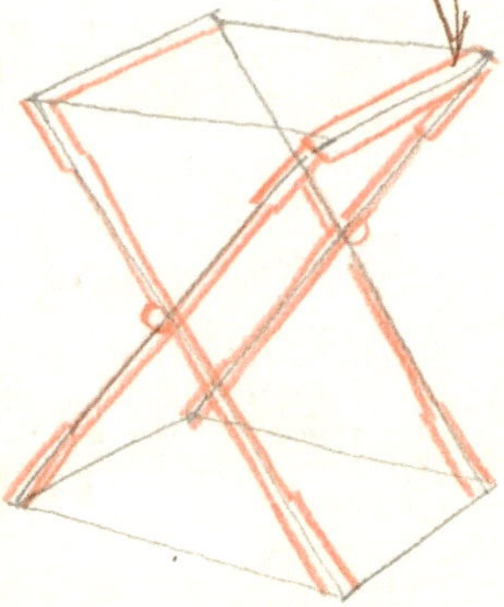

Add the fabric seat.

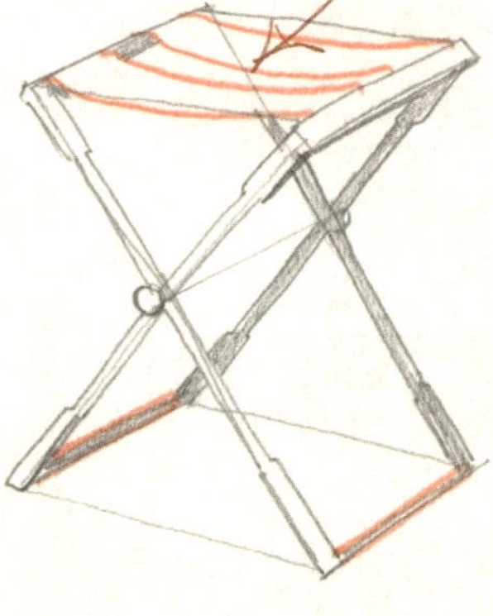

Draw an oval lozenge shape. Add three lines for legs.

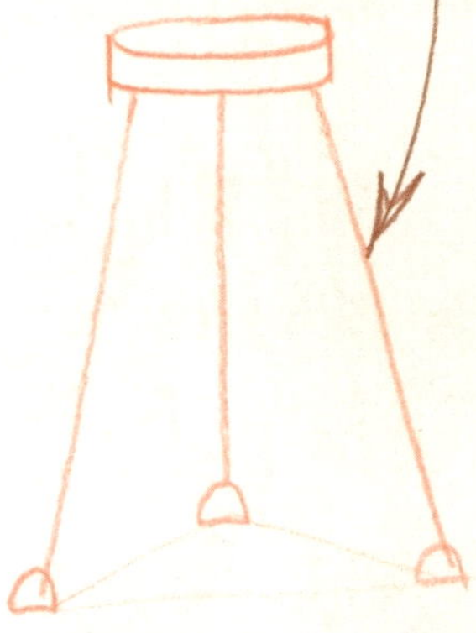

Draw in shaped, decorative legs.

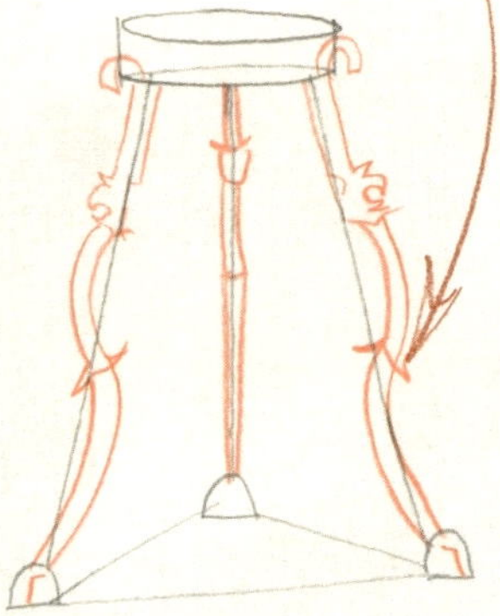

Add shade to areas light wouldn't reach.

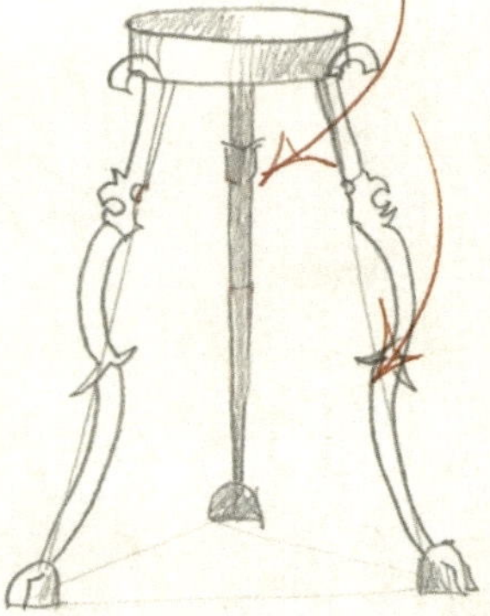

Erase any unwanted construction lines.

Try drawing the furniture within a Roman home scene.

ROMAN HOUSES

Ancient Greeks were the greatest influence on Roman architecture. The Romans were great innovators, adopting new construction materials and techniques which led to their innovative designs.

The Romans recognised the potential of using lime mortar to produce concrete. Concrete and rubble had already been used to fill hollow spaces but Roman architects realised that concrete could support great weight and be used to create a whole range of new architectural structures, such as a basilica, a triumphal arch, aqueducts, amphitheatres, granary buildings and tenement buildings.

Panoramic view of the houses and streets in the ancient city of Pompeii in Naples, Italy. This Roman city was destroyed by the eruption of Mount Vesuvius in the 1st century AD.

Herculaneum, Campania, Italy: the remains of Herculaneum following the eruption of Vesuvius in 79 AD.

Ruins of Herculaneum.

HOW TO DRAW ROMAN HOUSES

The Roman house was enclosed, with only a few windows in the outer walls for security and to cut out noise, dirt and smells from the street.

Draw a smaller rectangular box alongside (as shown).

Draw a simple square box.

Divide the wall in half.

Draw the top inward-sloping roof.

Now draw a smaller sloping roof inside the courtyard.

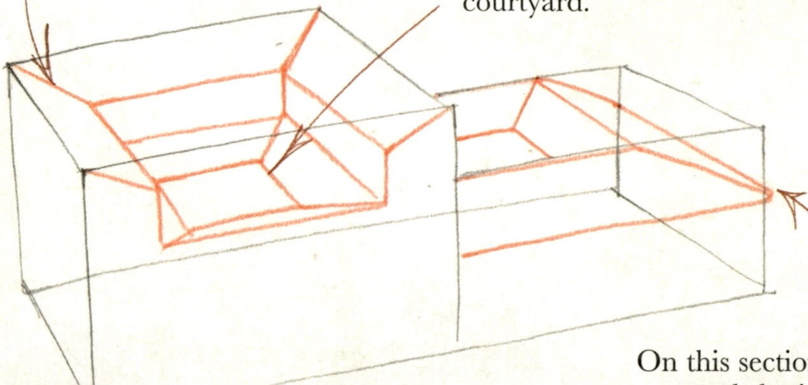

On this section draw an outward-sloping roof.

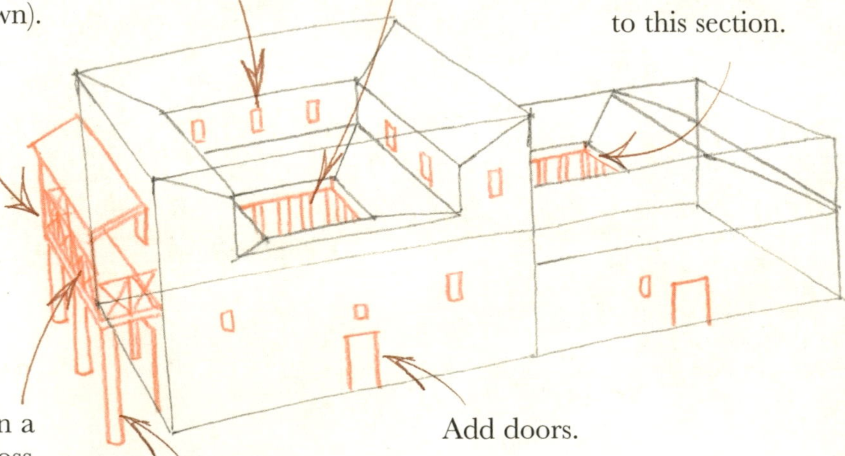

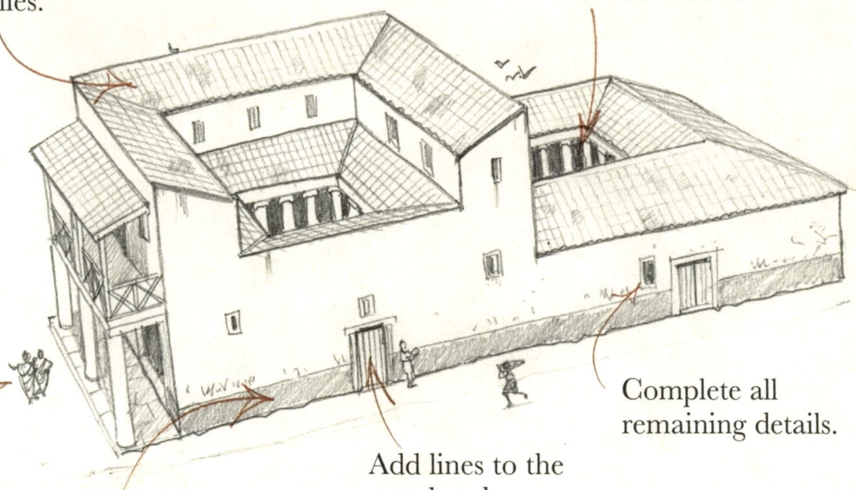

Erase any unwanted construction lines.

HADRIAN'S WALL

Stretching 117 kilometres (73 miles) from the coast of the Solway Firth to the North Sea, Hadrian's Wall was built to guard the north-west frontier of the Roman Empire. With the building of Hadrian's wall between 120–130 AD, defence of the northernmost part of the Roman empire became much easier.

Part of the ruins of Hadrian's Wall.

Draw the hills in the background.

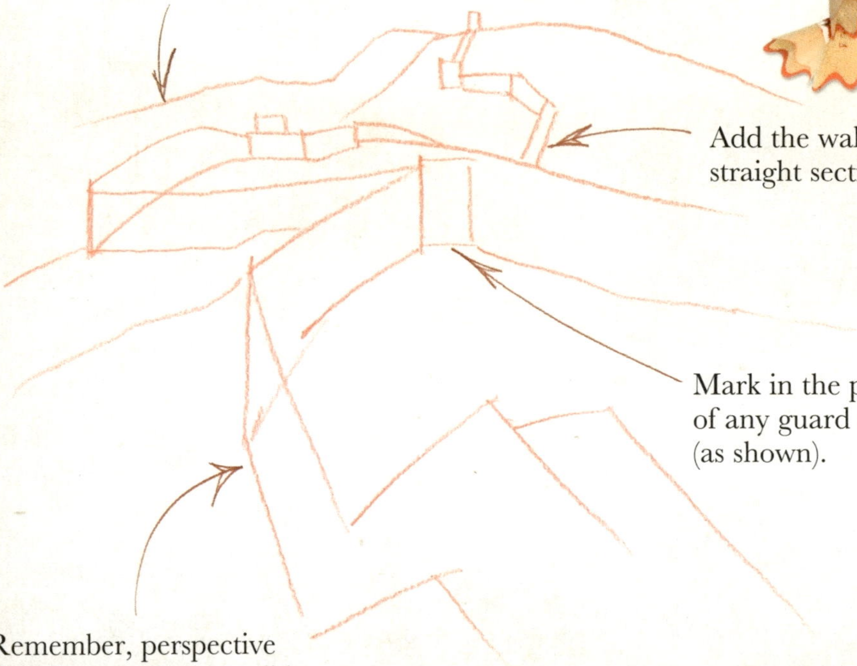

Add the wall in small straight sections.

Mark in the position of any guard towers (as shown).

Remember, perspective drawing means the wall is larger in the foreground.

Draw in the larger fortifications on the wall.

Add rugged lines to suggest the site.

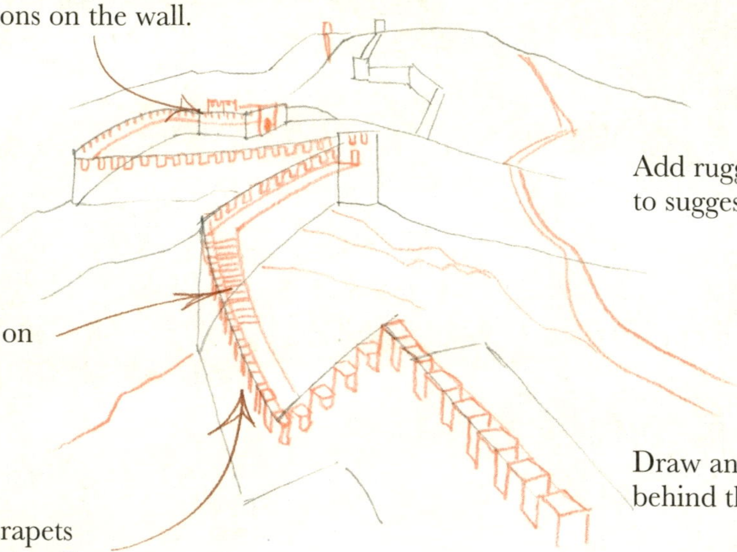

Draw in steps on the wall path.

Draw another path behind the wall.

Draw in parapets on top of the wall.

Complete all remaining details.

Add clouds.

Draw some Roman soldiers on the wall.

Decide on a light source and add shading to areas where light wouldn't reach.

Erase any unwanted construction lines.

GLOSSARY

Amphitheatre An oval arena, surrounded by seats where gladiator and wild beast shows were held.

Amphora A pottery jar for storing and carrying wine, olive oil and fish sauce.

Aqueduct A large bridge with a channel running across the top which brought water supplies into the town from the countryside.

Basilica Large public building, which served as the town hall and law courts.

Cameo A carving of a person's portrait or special symbol on a brooch or ring.

Citizens Roman males who had the right to vote to elect people to the Senate and to political posts in the Senate. They also had the right to wear a toga and serve as a legionary in the army.

Consul The highest political post in the time of the Republic. Two consuls were elected each year. They managed the senate's affairs and commanded the army.

Cult A religious movement or system centered around a particular figure or object.

Forum A town's central meeting and market place. The town's most important buildings and temples were usually in the forum.

Hadrian's Wall A fortified wall built in the north of England to protect the northwest frontier of the Roman Empire from attack.

Lararium A small shrine in a Roman house where statues

of the household gods were kept. The family worshipped at this shrine every day.

Merchant Someone who makes money by buying and selling wares.

Mosaic A wall or floor decoration made of broken pieces of tile or glass set in plaster.

Pantheon A Roman temple, now a church, in Rome, with a domed roof with a circular opening onto the sky. It is a famous example of ancient Roman architecture.

Patrician A member of one of the ruling class of families in ancient Rome.

Plebeians The word for a commoner in ancient Rome.

Provinces Areas outside Rome, which the Romans had conquered and now ruled. The rest of Italy was thought to be a province of Rome.

Triclinium The dining room of a house.

Underworld Also known as Hades, this was where a dead person's spirit was thought to go to be judged, before going on to Elysium (heaven) or Tartarus (hell).

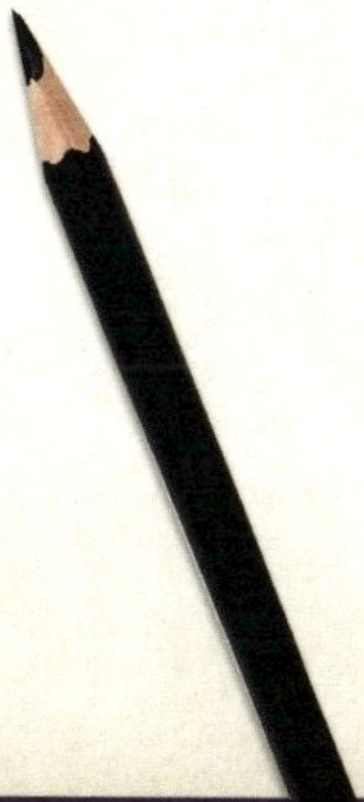

INDEX